T0266873

Disappointing Affirmations

by **Dave Tarnowski**

CHRONICLE BOOKS
SAN FRANCISCO

Library of Congress Cataloging-in-Publication Data available.

ISBN 978-1-7972-2666-8

Manufactured in China.

Photographs by Dave Tarnowski.
Design by Evelyn Furuta.

10 9 8 7

Chronicle books and gifts are available at special quantity discounts
to corporations, professional associations, literacy programs, and
other organizations. For details and discount information, please
contact our premiums department at corporatesales@chronicle-
books.com or at 1-800-759-0190.

Chronicle Books LLC
680 Second Street
San Francisco, California 94107
www.chroniclebooks.com

For anyone who doesn't feel seen.

Introduction

Everyone wants you to be okay. Many don't care if you actually are—they just want you to pretend to be okay when you're around them. Feelings make people uncomfortable, especially sadness, anguish, and grief; most people don't know how to deal with those. Not in any helpful way, at least.

Negative thoughts should be examined, not chased away. Affirmations must not be things reserved purely for positivity. "Negative" feelings need affirming too.

That's why I started making and sharing these Disappointing Affirmations. By making light of the negative thoughts we all have, I'm shining a light into the darkness where these scary things live and trying to show that they're not so scary after all, nor are they unfamiliar. I'm inviting people who suffer in silence to feel seen, to look at a Disappointing Affirmation and say, "That's me."

I didn't intend for these to be a counterweight to "toxic positivity" when I started writing them. I have bipolar disorder and ADHD and probably other stuff buried beneath those two behemoths. I've always felt a bit disconnected from the "regular" world. I've lived with severe depression and anxiety and unpredictable mood swings for most of my life, so I'm very familiar with the darkness—the darkness of feeling completely alone. And yet I'm far from alone, something that took me years to see. I was just one of many (many, many, many) who felt the same exact things. It took most of my life, but I finally learned how to feel less alone, and part of that was peering into the darkness and learning how to understand it and over time live with it. I did that by writing about it and eventually sharing it with the world in the hope of reaching others who feel like I do.

And nothing takes the power away from a fear like looking at it straight on—especially seeing it in type, in a serene photographic setting.

Fun fact: I took all the photographs for the Disappointing Affirmations myself, on vacations with my then-wife. Little did I know at the time that they would be the idyllic backgrounds for these little, necessary moments of acknowledging thoughts that so many of us share and that feel important to recognize, and yes, to laugh at.

Making light by shining light.

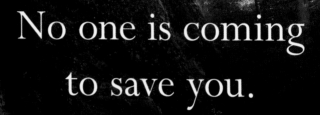

No one is coming
to save you.

You are the adult.

I'm so sorry.

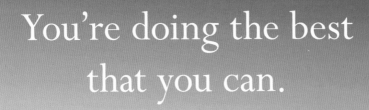

You're doing the best that you can.

Which is pretty sad.

The only person you can truly rely on is you.

What a fucking nightmare.

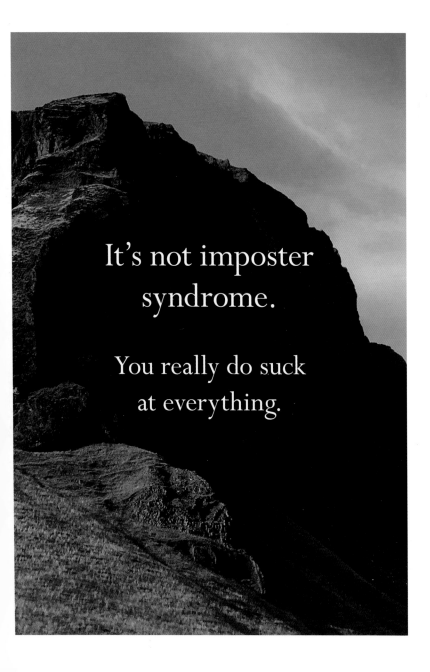

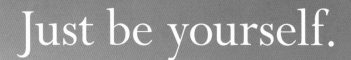

Just be yourself.

But not your real self.

No one wants to see that shit.

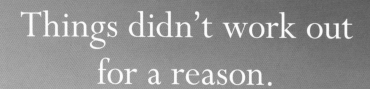

Things didn't work out
for a reason.

The reason is you make
terrible decisions.

Whenever someone asks how you are, just make up a lie like: "I'm okay."

No one wants to hear about your problems.

Stop worrying about what other people think.

I mean, have you met other people?

They're awful.

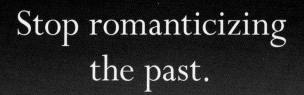

Stop romanticizing
the past.

You've always been
miserable.

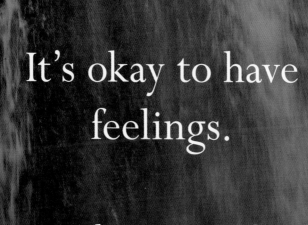

It's okay to have feelings.

But do you need to have so many?

Have a panic atta

. You've earned it.

Prioritize your mental health.

Have a good cry every morning
as you question everything
about your life.

Take a moment to be grateful
for all that you have.

Okay, now back to wishing
everything was different.

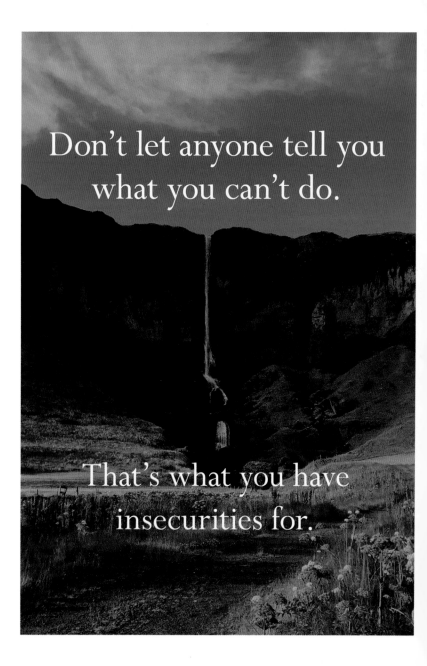

The life you want is outside your comfort zone.

So I guess you'll be sticking with this one, then.

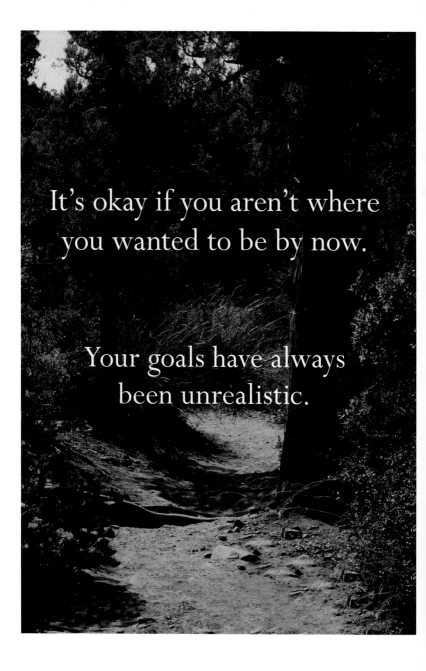

It's okay if you aren't where you wanted to be by now.

Your goals have always been unrealistic.

Be proud of yourself for how far you've come.

Especially considering that you've only ever done the bare minimum.

You ca

But you pr

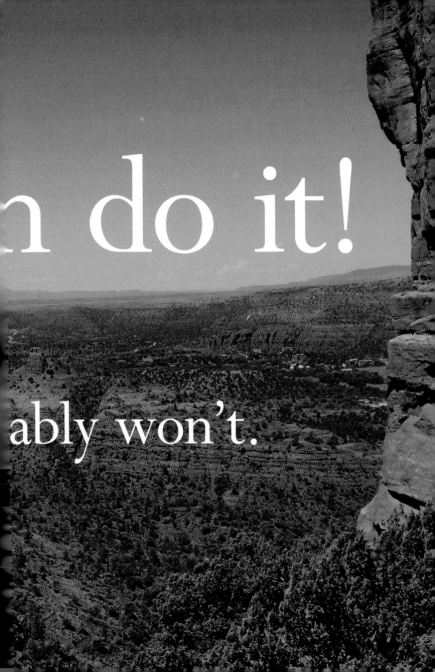

n do it!

ably won't.

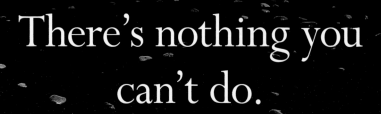

There's nothing you can't do.

As long as it doesn't have to be any good.

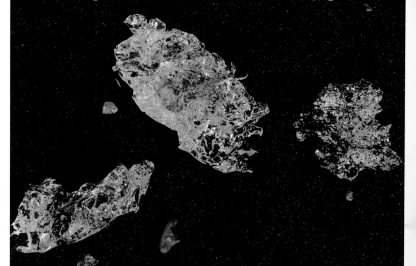

Don't be afraid
to try new things.

Like maybe getting
your shit together.

Why do something right away when you can wait for it to give you crippling anxiety?

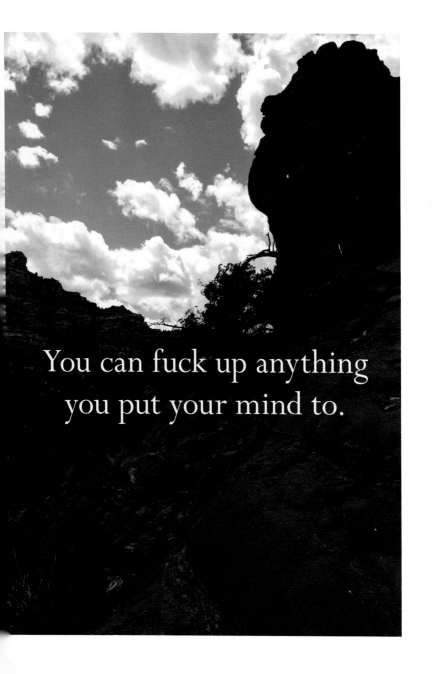

You can fuck up anything
you put your mind to.

Don't let anyone make you feel bad about yourself.

That's your job.

And nobody does it better.

Ask the universe
for guidance.

Then just go and do
whatever stupid shit
you were going
to do anyway.

The best way to cope with your problems is to add new ones to distract yourself from the original ones.

Self-Sabotage

Why wait for things to fail when you can make it happen?

Mistakes are how we learn.

It's why I make the same ones again and again.

I keep getting better at them.

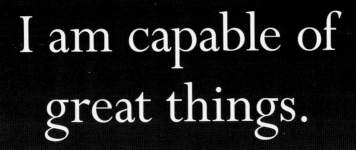

I am capable of great things.

I'm not going to actually do any of them, but I could.

Disappointed?

That's what you get for
expecting things.

Failure is alv

ys an option.

My entire vibe is
I don't want to.

I am only saying yes to things that spark joy.

If only I ever felt any joy.

I will not lose control
of my emotions.

I lost that shit a long time ago.

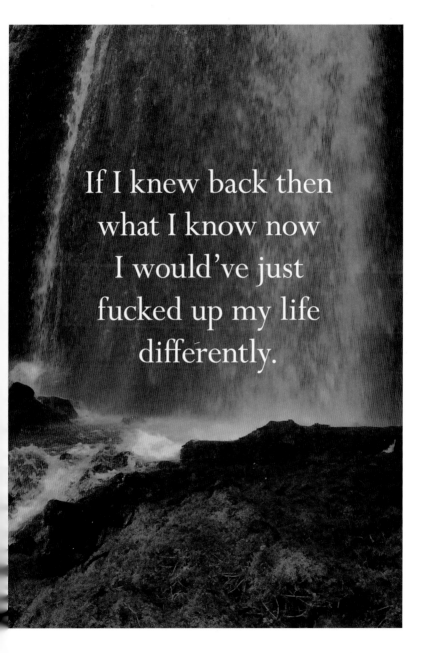

If I knew back then
what I know now
I would've just
fucked up my life
differently.

It's never too late
to change.

So just wait until you
absolutely have to.

Sometimes I gaze into the abyss
just so I can feel something
gaze back at me.

You will never
be alone.

All of the stupid things
you've ever said and
done will always be
there to haunt you.

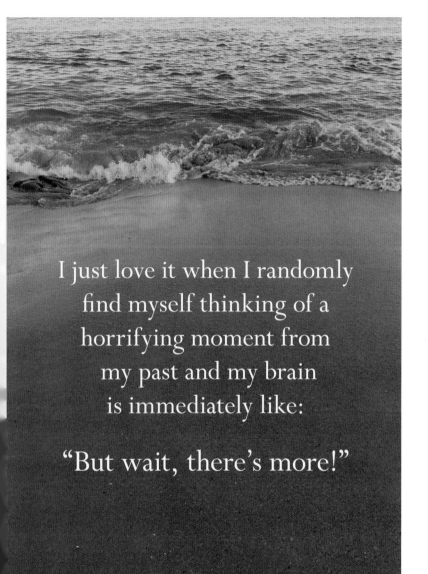

I just love it when I randomly
find myself thinking of a
horrifying moment from
my past and my brain
is immediately like:

"But wait, there's more!"

Give yourself a

eak. Dissociate.

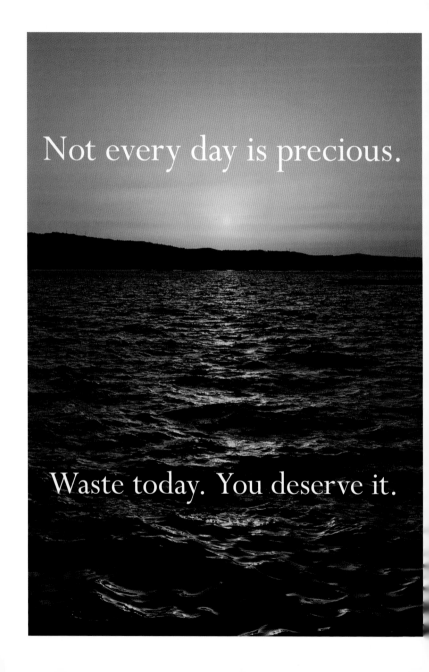

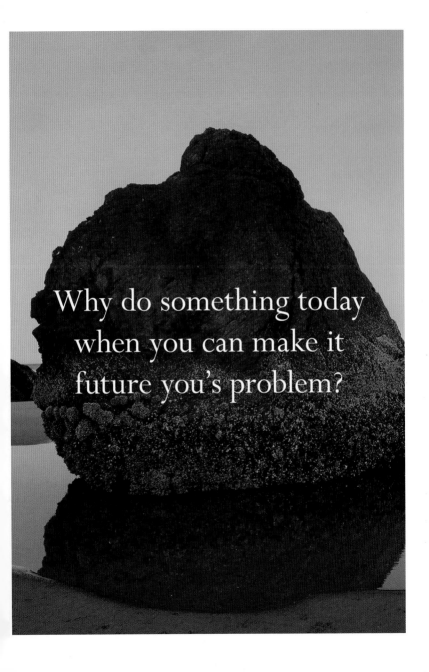

Why do something today when you can make it future you's problem?

I am exactly where
I want to be.

At home, avoiding people.

People come into our lives
for a reason.

Sometimes that reason
is to make us enjoy
being alone.

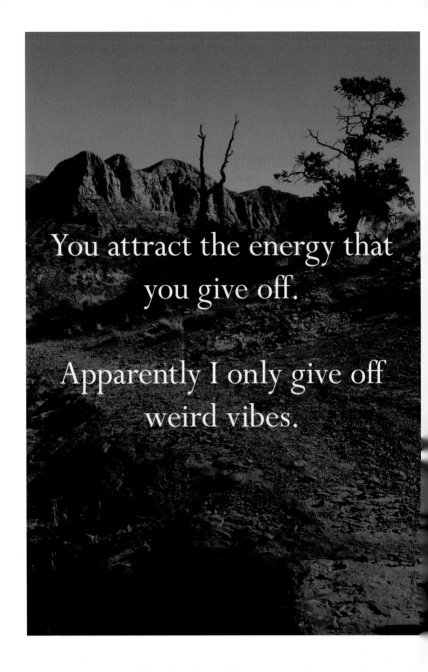

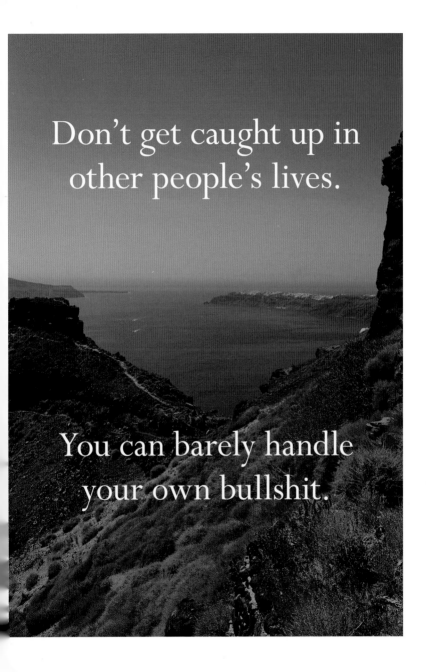

A person's true nature
is revealed when something
takes a few seconds longer
than it normally does.

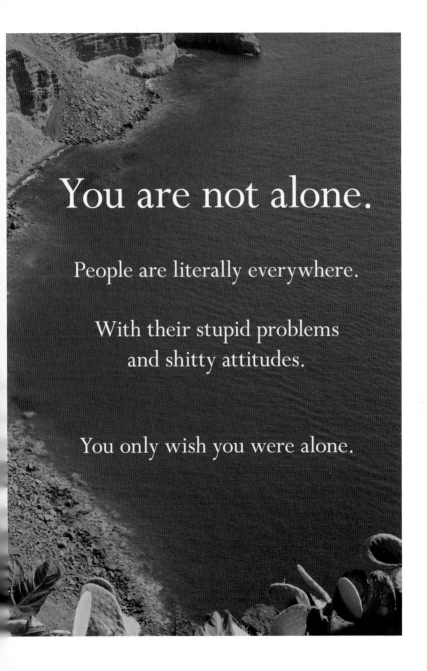

Every now and
the top of you

hen, scream at
ungs. It helps.

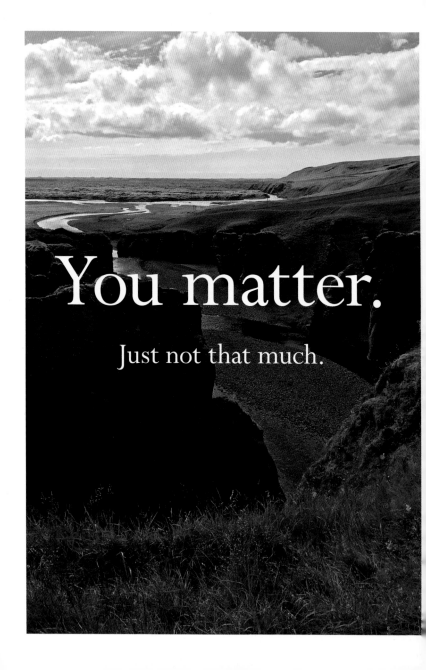

Never forget who the fuck you are.

Because most people have no idea you exist.

You are more than enough.

Way more.

Dial that shit back a bit.

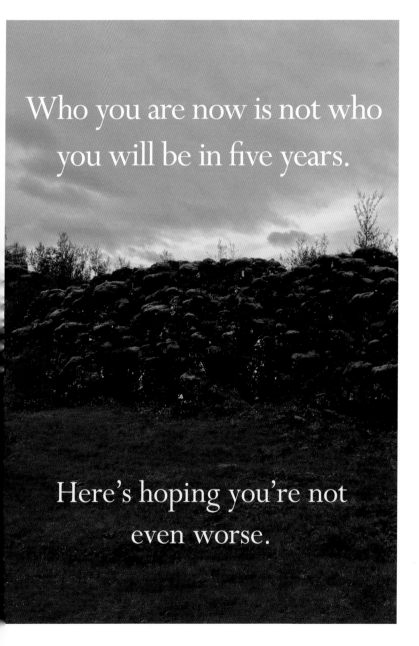

Who you are now is not who you will be in five years.

Here's hoping you're not even worse.

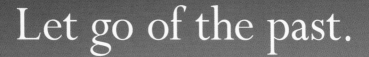

Let go of the past.

You're holding yourself back
from making new regrets.

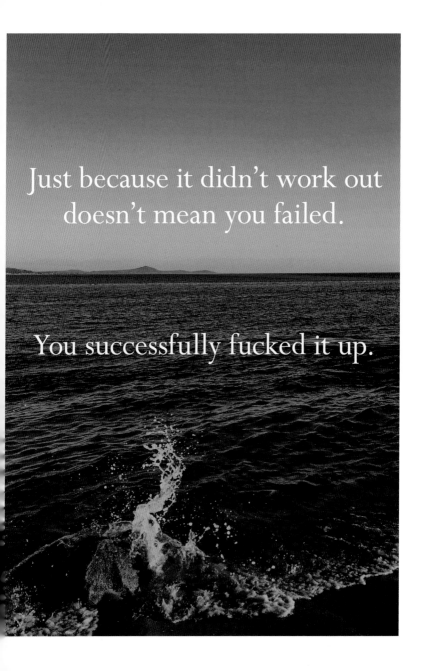

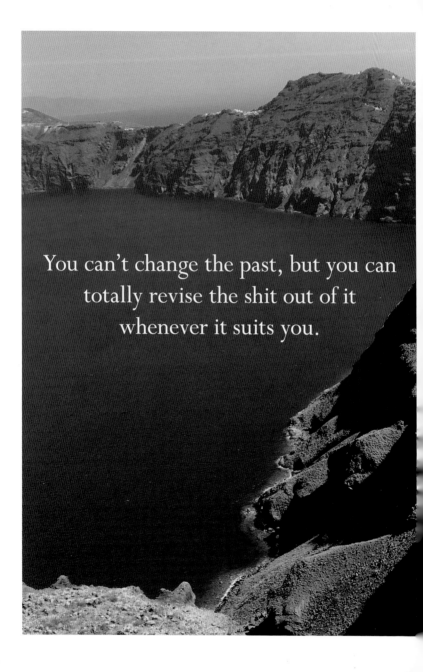

You can't change the past, but you can totally revise the shit out of it whenever it suits you.

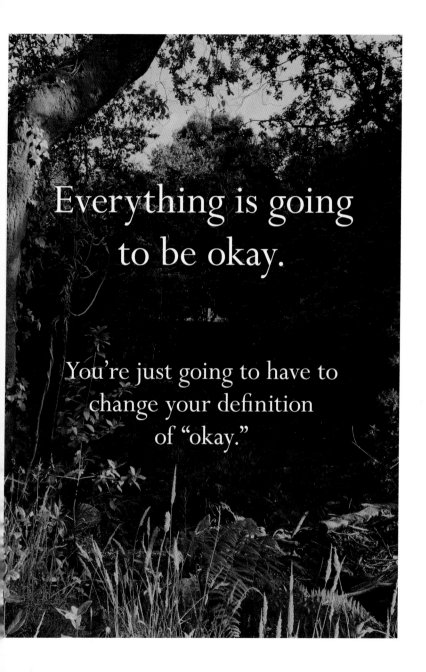

Today I am only focusing on things that truly matter.

Like shit that happened in the past that I can do nothing to change.

There's so much life out there just waiting to be discovered.

But there's also tons of good shit to binge-watch at home.

Each new d
can't return
that you

is a gift you

r something

ally want.

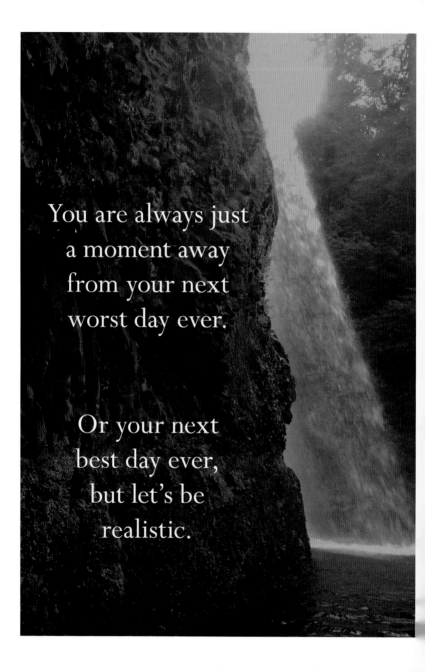

You are always just
a moment away
from your next
worst day ever.

Or your next
best day ever,
but let's be
realistic.

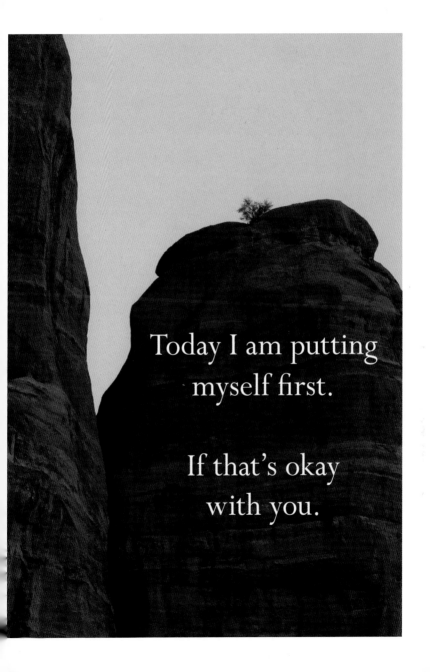

Today I am putting
myself first.

If that's okay
with you.

To love and be loved in return is the greatest thing there is.

But plans being canceled at the last minute is a close second.

Don't say yes out of guilt.

Say, "Yes, out of guilt."

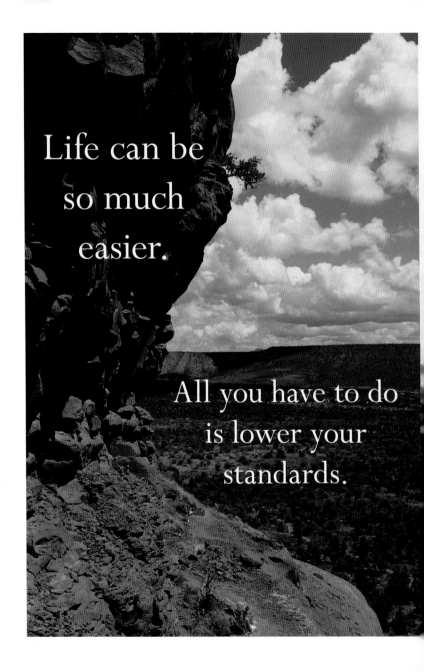

You can be anything
that you want.

And yet you keep choosing
to be you.

I admire your dedication
to the role.

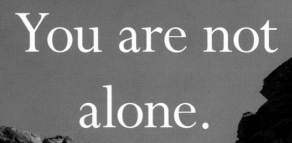

You are not
alone.

Everyone else is
disappointed
in you too.

Try something today
that scares you.

Like maybe doing the dishes or
the laundry or returning a
phone call or leaving
the house or …

Fuck it, t

ke a nap.

From now on I will only make good decisions.

Honestly, I shouldn't even be allowed to make any of my own decisions.

Don't be afraid to settle.

I mean, have you met you?

This too shall pass.

And then some other bullshit
will come and take its place.

It never fucking ends.

Today I am letting go
of the things that are
holding me back
from the life that
I want to live.

Then I'm picking them all
up again because I have
separation anxiety.

Be kind to yourself, asshole.

Actual photo of the hole
where I stuff all of
my feelings.

Accept you

hot mess

self for the

at you are.

Acknowledgments

I'd like to thank the following people,
in no particular order: me, for still being
here; my family (most of them);
my friends (both real and imaginary);
my two ex-wives (so far);
all of my therapists; my agent; my editor
and the whole Chronicle team;
and above all, you.